Axel Gutjahr

Setting Up an
Aquarium

Everything About
Purchase, Care,
and Nutrition

BARRON'S

Contents

Aquariums for Beginners

With an aquarium you bring a piece of nature into your home: a living, fascinating underwater world at eye level that will bring you newfound joys every day. There are virtually no limits to your personal creativity when setting up your aquarium. Everything you need to know for an easy start is provided to you in this book.

How It All Began

In 1856, when natural scientist Emil Adolf Ross-mässler published an article in the then popular magazine *Die Gartenlaube* (*The Summerhouse*) entitled "Der See im Glase" ("The Sea in a Glass Jar"), he had no idea that he would be laying the foundation for the concept of proper aquarium care. In fact, with that particular publication, the principle of modern-day aquarium keeping started its triumphant march to popularity. Since then, keeping an aquarium has inspired and entertained millions of people worldwide.

The Aquarium Today

For many people, the particular fascination of an aquarium lies in the fact that it enables them to view the world of fish underwater, and from a totally different perspective than is possible in nature. For most of us, aquariums also have a distinctly relaxing effect. After a stressful day at work, many aquarium hobbyists make it a habit to relax for a few minutes in front of their aquarium and observe the lively behavior of their fish. Beyond that, an attractively decorated and meticulously maintained aquarium also contributes significantly to the aesthetics of the living space in any home.

Aquarium Dreams Come True

You may have been thinking for a long time of getting such a miniature underwater world for your living room. In fact, for many people this is often the fulfillment of a childhood dream. This book will accompany you on the path to your dream aquarium and give you the basic, essential aquarium knowledge. We will show you, step-by-step, all that is required to set up and decorate a great aquarium effectively. You will avoid making big mistakes, and right from the start you will have a lot of fun with your new hobby.

Costs at a Glance

START-UP COSTS	APPROX. PRICE
Aquarium 40 × 20 × 16 inch	$140
Aquarium cabinet	$200–$350
External filter 92–106 gal/hr	$100
Heater w/thermostat	$35–$110
Cover with 1–2 light bars	$70–$100
With 2–4 fluorescent tubes	$40–$85
Tank background structure	$15–$70
Substrate (gravel, sand)	$15–$30
Rocks, roots, bamboo tubes, caves	$30–$140
Small equipment items, such as nets, feeding rings, tubifex trap, siphon hose, sponge or glass cleaner	$30–$60
Water plants	$70–$140
Fish	$140
ONGOING OPERATIONS COSTS	
Water for weekly partial water change (approx. nine gal)	Variable depending on location
Electricity costs	Depending on local rates and usage by equipment
Food, medication (occasionally), filter components	$4–$5 per week
Water plant fertilizer	$15–$20
Replacements for water plants and/or fish	$15

How Expensive Is an Aquarium?

It is important to consider costs. Distinguish between the one-time costs for the actual purchase of the tank (including stand or cabinet), the essential life-support equipment (filter, heater, pumps, lights, etc.), and the ongoing operating costs for the operation of an aquarium. Certain costs can actually recur after a few years, mostly for replacement purchases, such as a new pump or heater. It may indeed be more expensive to repair broken or faulty equipment than to purchase new equipment. The accompanying table gives you an overview of the approximate costs for basic aquarium equipment. I strongly recommend you get estimated prices from several aquarium stores or pet shops before the actual purchase.

Opportunities for Savings

Certain cost savings can be achieved with some of the required items. Instead of a dedicated aquarium cabinet to support the tank, you can also use a stable piece of furniture, such as a chest of drawers or a sideboard. You can collect gravel or sand from a local sand or gravel pit and gather or dig up rocks or suitable pieces of roots, too. The points you need to observe with these do-it-yourself activities are outlined on page 11. You can also make rock caves as hiding places for your fish yourself. Bamboo sticks and tubes, cut to the required lengths, can be bought from building suppliers or garden nurseries at a reasonable cost. Water plants and fish are often available cheaper from aquarium exchanges (often held at regular intervals by local aquarium clubs) than from retail aquarium or pet stores. Moreover, you can even save money on fish food, for instance, by catching it yourself. (See page 44.)

Types of Aquariums

A few decades ago, frame aquariums were the most commonly used aquarium type. They consisted of a welded metal frame into which glass panels were secured with putty. Another older type of aquarium is the all-glass tank, poured from molten glass in one piece. This type of tank is currently undergoing a certain renaissance in the form of goldfish bowls; however, generally I advise against using them. These bulbous-shaped tanks with a relatively small opening at the top do not really fulfill the requirements for proper, species-correct maintenance of aquarium fish.

In the meantime, metal frame tanks have been replaced nearly everywhere by tanks where the glass sides have been bonded together directly to each other using a silicone sealant.

Diversity of Shapes

Silicon-sealed tanks are available in the aquarium trade (pet shops and dedicated aquarium shops) in a variety of different shapes. There are not only traditional, cube-shaped models, but also triangular (corner) tanks, as well as aquariums with concave and convex sides. The latter have a serious disadvantage—in such tanks, the shapes of fish always appear distorted. Tall aquariums, with hexagonal or octagonal glass panels at the bottom, are often placed on columns or pedestals. However, such tanks often hold a large volume of water, yet the water surface area is relatively small. This impedes gas exchange between the water surface and the air above, which can lead to an oxygen deficiency in the water. Such tanks are really only suitable for keeping labyrinth (air-breathing) fish, which can "breathe" supplementary, atmospheric air at the tank's surface.

An Important Point to Remember

Make sure that all sides are free of external scratches and do not contain tiny internal air bubbles within the glass, and that the sides and the bottom panel are bonded securely to each other.

Halogen lamps are very useful for illuminating open aquariums when freely suspended from above.

The Correct Location for Your Aquarium

Before you purchase your aquarium, it is important to find a suitable location in your home for the tank. Normally, you would probably like to have your aquarium directly in front of you, at eye level when sitting down. The aquarium should become the focal point and principal attraction in your home, at least of the area it's in. At the same time, it is also important that all necessary service and maintenance tasks can be done unimpeded. Lastly, the stability of the tank and the stand or cabinet must be assured. Within this context you need to be aware that a tank with (for instance) a volume of 50 gal (200 l) and filled with substrate and various decorative items often weighs 660–770 lbs. (300–350 kg)! Positioning a tank next to a window with a southern exposure is not suitable because the intensive sunshine favors the growth of green algae. On the other hand, locating a tank in the proximity of a window facing east or west is far better, because there the daily exposure to direct sunlight is far less.

An Open Aquarium

Operating an aquarium without a cover–an "open tank"–is done principally for visual effect. Well-kept open aquariums look very attractive and are a genuine jewel in a home. You can also integrate terrestrial indoor plants in the decorative design of an open aquarium; for instance, Devil's Ivy (*Epipremnum*), often referred to as *Philodendron*, can be kept in the back section of such an aquarium, in a manner similar to hydroculture. Nitrogenous and phosphorous compounds present in aquarium water are sufficient for the nutrition of these plants. The aesthetic effect of these terrestrial plants can be enhanced beautifully with various water plants, for instance, the *Echinodorus* species, with leaves that often develop above the water surface.

When you have found the ideal location for your aquarium, your attractively planted and decorated tank will become a fascinating focal point in your home.

Fish in an Open Aquarium

FISH THAT WILL JUMP READILY: Guppies (*Poecilia reticulata*) belong to a group of fish species that will readily jump out of the water when startled. They are unsuitable for an open aquarium due to the danger that they will actually jump out of the tank and end up on the floor of the living room, where they will inevitably die.

SUITABLE FISH: Well-suited for open tanks are, for instance, Dwarf Gouramis (*Colisa lalia*), Pearl Gouramis (*Trichogaster leeri*), and Corydoras catfish (*Corydoras* sp.). These are all slow-swimming species that are never hyperactive. Equally suitable for an open aquarium are Red Neon Tetras (*Paracheirodon axelrodi*) and Flame Tetras (*Hyphessobrycon flammeus*).

Biological Balance

Your aquarium will function properly only after a well-defined biological balance between animals, plants, and microorganisms has become established. This biological balance is being maintained by a cycle of interactions. Within this cycle, a multitude of microorganisms that have become established in the substrate, as well as in the filter, break down various metabolic (excretory) products given off by the animals in the aquarium and turn them into substances that are nutrients for water plants. The plants, in turn, produce oxygen required by the fish for respiration. Moreover, water plants in an aquarium also contribute to the biological balance by competing with algae for nutrients dissolved in the aquarium water. This competition then limits the development of algae.

Large Beats Small

Many beginning aquarium hobbyists believe that small tanks are easier to maintain than large ones, but this is NOT true! In fact, exactly the opposite is the case. Large tanks can actually be maintained with smaller maintenance efforts, because the larger water volume provides for greater environmental stability.

When Aquarium Conditions Are Disrupted

In overcrowded aquarium conditions (too many fish), the biological balance of the tank becomes disrupted: an accumulated excess of nutrients occurs that can lead to an explosion of algae growth, which can then sometimes also become attached to plant leaves in the aquarium. Consequently, the photosynthetic capacity of water plants is decreased. They can no longer grow properly and their leaves will die. When this happens, there is only one way out; you must reduce the number of fish dramatically and start effective algae eradication methods (see page 52). During the summer months, excessive exposure of the tank to sunlight can also be the cause of too much algae.

Variegated [or Variable] Platys (*Xipohophorus variatus*) occur in many captive-bred varieties of this species.

Substrate and Decoration

The bottom substrate of an aquarium is not only a decorative element in the underwater landscape, but it also fulfils other important functions. The roots of water plants are anchored in the substrate, and they also find essential nutrients there. Moreover, the substrate also acts as the habitat for many useful microorganisms; some species even use the material on the bottom of the aquarium for spawning purposes.

Sand and gravel: A substrate made up of a slightly clayish mixture of sand and gravel is suitable for most community aquariums. When selecting it, you need to make sure that the gravel grains are less than a quarter-inch (about 6 mm) in diameter; the individual grains must not have sharp edges that could lead to injuries when, for instance, barbs or catfish forage for food along and in the substrate. I also recommend the use of dark colored gravel. The coloration of most fish will take on deeper color tones and seem more intense once the aquarium is fully operational and has a dark substrate.

Laterite: Another commonly used substrate is *laterite*, which is a material that originates in the tropics. It is generally available from aquarium shops. The reddish to reddish brown coloration of laterite is due to high concentrations of iron oxide in this material, which also has a positive effect on the growth of many plant species.

Rocks assembled to form caves must always be glued together with silicon sealant so that they do not collapse.

Coconut shells are preferred hiding and spawning places for many fish.

Peat Moss: Many fish species (e.g., egg-laying tooth-carps) require at least some areas along the bottom of the aquarium with a layer of peat moss up to four inches (10 cm) thick. The fish use this material as spawning substrate where they deposit their eggs. Use the special aquarium peat moss available from an aquarium store; however, peat lowers the pH of the water, which means the water can become too acidic (for more about pH values, see pages 16–17). Therefore, you should always monitor the pH of the aquarium water when using peat to make sure that the pH does not drop too far. You can raise the pH by mixing some finely ground limestone (calcium carbonate) in with the substrate. You can make this material yourself simply by smashing some calcium carbonate rocks with a hammer; alternately, this material is available from aquarium or pet shops. Calcium carbonate containing substrates which produce an alkaline pH are preferred by fish from the Rift Valley Lakes of East Africa (e.g., the cichlids from that region) or those from the Yucatan Peninsula (Mexico), such as live-bearing swordtails.

Aquarium Decoration

Rocks: Rocks of different shapes and sizes are among the most frequently used items of decoration in an aquarium. Yet, you must not select specimens that contain mineral or metallic inclusions, for instance, those particular rocks that you can recognize by the presence of glittering or vitreous (glass-like) inclusions. Similarly, you must not use rocks with sharp edges, because these can cause injuries to the fish.

Flat, plate-like rocks can be useful for erecting and constructing caves and castles; however, so that such manmade structures do not collapse

Roots give your underwater world a rather original and nature-like appearance.

when fish come in contact with them (or dig underneath), I advise you to glue the individual rocks together, using silicon sealant. For such purposes, you should always use special aquarium silicon. Other types of silicon contain components which are toxic to fish.

Slate tiles, which are often placed flat onto the substrate, are also very popular, but a word of caution: the fracture lines on slate tiles can also be very sharp and cause injuries to fish, just like rocks with sharp edges, In order to avoid this hazard, you should smooth out these fracture lines/edges with sandpaper or a file.

Roots: Banks of rivers and streams and other shallow bodies of water can readily be recreated in an aquarium using tree roots or gnarled pieces of natural wood. Apart from bogwood roots (available in the aquarium trade), water-soaked roots from oak and alder trees or from grapevines are also use-ful for that purpose. How you have to treat these roots before you can use them in an aquarium will be explained on page 25. Beyond that, aquarium shops nearly always offer *Mopani* wood from a tropical Africa for the very same pur-pose. Just like the types of roots mentioned earlier, Mopani wood also takes decades to decompose and barely ever shows any signs of decay.

Coconut shells: Coconuts are a characteristic fruit of the tropics, and are very popular as decoration in an aquarium. One or two coconut half-shells (with the meat already removed), partially buried in the substrate, will give your aquarium landscape a particular attraction. Many fish like coconut shells as hiding places or spawning caves.

Bamboo: Similarly decorative are bamboo sticks and tubes. Bamboo tubes can be glued horizon-tally onto a slate tile, which is then placed on the substrate. Bamboo tubes presented in this manner

You can use bamboo very effectively for decorating an aquarium. So that the cut end of each bamboo stick does not decay, coat the cut surfaces with silicon sealant.

are eagerly accepted by various locariid catfish (family Locariidae) as caves and general hiding places. Bamboo sticks should be placed more or less vertically in an aquarium, simply by pushing one end into the substrate. In order to prevent them from drifting back up to the surface, it is advisable to attach them with silicone to some rocks. If you coat the cut ends of the bamboo sticks with a thin silicone layer, it will prevent decay bac-teria from becoming established on these surfaces.

Leaves: Some of the dwarf cichlids seem to feel most comfortable with the substrate in an aquar-ium, when it is at least partially covered with fallen leaves. Instead of oak or beech leaves—a common choice for some time—dried palm leaves (often available from garden nurseries), are even better suited for a tropical underwater world. Before you can place leaves into your aquarium, they need to be washed in warm water. Then you put them in a container with water and weigh them down with a rock. After a day or so the leaves will have become saturated with water so that they remain on the bottom; they can then be used in an aquarium.

Background decoration: To hide the area in back of the aquarium, you can use either a plastic sheet with a printed underwater landscape on it, or a nature-like recreation as a plastic relief, simulating an underwater embankment of a stream or lake. You attach the printed plastic sheet to the outside of the aquarium's back panel (print facing in to the aquarium), and the plastic relief structure is placed actually inside the tank.

External (outside) filters have the advantage that they do not reduce the actual water volume in the aquarium through displacement. Moreover, they are very easy to service.

Basic Equipment Required

The aquarium trade offers a very large assortment of technical equipment for your aquarium. The following appliances are essential to service the basic needs of an aquarium: filter, heater, and lighting. The filter is usually combined with an aerator, which facilitates continuous water circulation throughout the tank. In contrast to filters operating inside the aquarium, external filters have proven to be more effective because they do not have an impact through displacement on the volume of aquarium water. Particularly maintenance-friendly are outside filters where the in- and outflow pipe can be closed off with a separate valve. This way you avoid any unnecessary mess when opening the filter. You should select a heater that includes a contact thermometer (thermostat), so you can set the required temperature only once without having to make any subsequent adjustments. In contrast to rod heaters attached by suction cups (preferably in a corner of the tank), bottom heaters are installed under the substrate. Although bottom heaters are generally somewhat more expensive, they offer the advantage that they warm all water layers in the aquarium. This way, even the water plants will never get "cold feet"; this has a positive effect on their growth.

Aquarium shops also offer combined heater-filter systems, where the water is heated as it flows through the filter. When there is an electrical fault with one or the other component of a unit, neither will work, and the entire system will need to be repaired or replaced.

Lighting

The lighting intensity and duration have significant impact on the growth and photosynthetic activity of water plants. An aquarium should be illuminated

on the average for 12 to 14 hours daily. The most commonly used light sources are fluorescent tubes screwed into a light bar inside the cover of the aquarium. In order to always assure adequate illumination, for, say, a tank 40 inches (100 cm) long and 16 inches (40 cm) wide, you should, if possible, install four 30-watt fluorescent tubes. The aquarium trade also offers fluorescent tubes specifically designed to meet the requirements of water plants. For the illumination of open aquariums it is often recommended to use high-pressure mercury vapor lamps, referred to as HQL and HQI lamps. These lamps are suspended from the ceiling 8–20 inches (20–50 cm) above the tank; they usually come with an attractive lampshade. One disadvantage of these lamps is their diminished degree of effectiveness, because they tend to convert a large amount of the electricity used into heat and not into light. Free-hanging fluorescent tubes in a modern-looking fitting are better suited for an open aquarium.

Other Technical Components

Apart from filters and heaters, the aquarium trade offers still other equipment items, but these are not necessarily required. Especially technically-inclined hobbyists tend to use equipment such as electronic testing devices for controlling the water chemistry parameters. These can be used not only to determine specific water values quickly, but also extremely accurately. Another special piece of equipment is the carbonator, which serves to add carbon dioxide to the water, as an added stimulant

Rod heaters in an aquarium assure that the water maintains the correct temperature, which is very important for the well-being of aquarium fish.

Two fluorescent tubes can be screwed into this aquarium cover, which will then illuminate the entire tank.

Hand nets are part of the essential accessories needed for keeping an aquarium.

for enhanced plant growth. Special enrichment of the aquarium water with oxygen can be achieved by using an oxidator. Aquarium filters with built-in ultraviolet sterilizers are used to kill disease-causing germs and suspended algae by passing the filtered water over an ultraviolet lamp housed within the same unit. You should seek detailed advice from your aquarium shop and then decide on what equipment will best assist you and what is available to you within your budget.

Accessories

Apart from the basic technical equipment, you will also need various small accessories required for routine care and maintenance work on your aquarium. You will have to purchase a siphoning hose of sufficient diameter to remove the accumulated debris along the bottom and for partial water changes, but one that is narrow enough to avoid fish being sucked through the hose. Furthermore, for emergencies you should have two or three hose

clamps at the ready. You can use a plastic sponge or a commercially available glass cleaner (also referred to as a glass scraper) for removing algae from the aquarium's glass sides. The essential aquarium (start-up) equipment needs to be completed with the purchase of two or three hand nets different mesh sizes, and possibly also a floating feeding ring or a ring with an inserted sieve for feeding *tubifex* (the so-called *tubifex* trap).

Aquarium Computer

Once you have acquired some aquarium experience, you can use an aquarium computer for adjusting and constant control of various water parameters; however, such a computer must be connected to the appropriate items of equipment. The computer can also then be used for simulating tropical (and therefore nature-like) sunrises and sunsets in your aquarium.

Some Elementary Water Chemistry

Fish are only comfortable in their watery habitat if the water quality is suitable for them. If you are going to use water straight from the tap for your aquarium, it must be clear and odorless to start with. Beyond that, the degree of acidity, the pH, and the so-called "softness" or "hardness" of the water are very important. You will need to determine and probably adjust both of these parameters so that your fish can act and interact normally.

The pH

The pH value shows whether aquarium water is *acidic*, *alkaline*, or *neutral*. Water with a pH of 7.0 is neutral; pH values lower than 7 are characteristic of acidic water, and we refer to water with a pH value above 7 as being alkaline (or *basic*).

Most commonly kept aquarium fish require pH values between 6.5 and 7.5 (more about this in the chapter on Fish Portraits on pages 34 to 39).

You can very quickly determine the pH of water using commercially available inexpensive test strips.

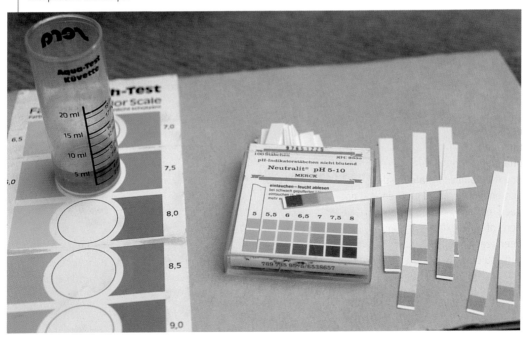

Determining the pH with test strips is child's play.

If the pH drops or increases outside this range, the habitat will become hostile to your fish. That can lead to inflammations of gills, fins, and scales.

You can easily measure the pH in your aquarium by using commercially available, inexpensive test strips. Apart from test strips, the aquarium trade also offers very precise electronic meters; however, these are not exactly cheap. Should you measure an elevated pH value, or one that is too low, you will have to make the appropriate adjustments (lower or higher) for the sake of your fish.

Quick Relief from a pH that Is too High

Values that are too high can be lowered with an extract made from seedpods of alder trees, oak bark chips, or from special aquarium peat moss. You can make this yourself: put two or three hand-fuls of seedpods, oak chips, or peat moss into a bucket and pour lukewarm water over this material. This is then left standing for 24 hours. Next day you decant the (by then) coffee-colored solution through a strainer. The liquid is then added in small quantities into the aquarium, while very gently stirring the aquarium water so that it becomes quickly and uniformly mixed in. Then—do not forget—you need to measure the pH between subsequent additions of the extract. As soon as a desired pH has been reached, stop adding the extract.

If you do not want to make your own pH-lowering extracts, you can also use numerous commercial products for that purpose available from the aquarium trade.

Ways to Increase the pH

An increase in pH can also be achieved merely by adding strong aeration to the aquarium, which then drives out and dissolves carbon dioxide (carbonic acid). For that you turn up filtration to the highest possible level until the pH in the aquarium has improved. In addition, you can also place a small cloth bag of ground-up limestone or shell grit in the filter canister. During the following hours and days you must check the water values regularly, and if need be, slow down filtration or remove the limestone as soon as the desired pH is reached. The pH value, expressed in Decadian Logarithms, is often interpreted incorrectly. An increase or decrease of the pH by a whole number means a tenfold adjustment of the acidity or alkalinity. For instance, water with a pH of 5.5 is 10 times as acidic as water with a pH of 6.5.

Water Hardness

The hardness of water is a measure of the calcium and magnesium compounds dissolved in it. You can distinguish between temporary hardness (determined by the dissolved carbonate compounds of calcium and magnesium) and non-carbonate hardness (a measure of the carbonate-free compounds of calcium and magnesium). Non-carbonate hardness and carbonate hardness together represent the total hardness, which is measured in degrees of General Hardness (dGH).

Many tropical fish species, which originally came from habitats with soft or very soft water, can also handle slightly higher degrees of hardness under aquarium conditions. The reason for this is that most tropical fish currently traded have been bred under aquarium conditions for generations, and they have therefore become adapted to slightly elevated hardness. Only when attempting to breed certain species will the same (or nearly the same) hardness prevalent in the original habitat of a particular species be required. Various, easy-to-use test kits for the determination of water hardness are available in the aquarium trade. According to the values that have been determined, water can be placed into the five categories in the table on this page.

Water Hardness at a Glance

dGH	Category
0–4	Very soft water
5–8	Soft water
9–14	Medium hard water
15–20	Hard water
21 and higher	Very hard water

The most important function of plants in an aquarium is the production of oxygen.

Elementary Physics of Water

The well-being of aquarium fish is also extremely dependent on water temperature. Depending on the species you are keeping, the temperature should be kept between 64 and 86°F (18–30°C) for tropical fish. While Zebra Fish (*Danio rerio*) and Rosy Barbs (*Puntius conchonius*), for instance, do best in slightly cooler water, 64–75°F (18–24°C), Harlequins (*Trigonostigma heteromorpha*) and Venezuelan Butterfly Cichlids (*Mikrogeophagus ramirezi*) require water temperatures of 75 to 84°F (24 to 29°C). You can find further details about temperature requirements of particular species in Fish Portraits on pages 34–39.

Here it must also be pointed out that with increasing water temperature, the maximum oxygen saturation capability of water decreases. For instance, water at 64°F (18°C) has a maximum saturation capacity that is almost 20 percent higher than that of water at 86°F (30°C). However, that does not present a real problem, provided the aquarium has abundant plant growth and it is not overcrowded with fish. At elevated temperatures, together with appropriate illumination, most tropical water plants increase their photosynthesis and give off more oxygen into the water. In order to maintain the oxygen content of aquarium water at optimum level, attach the discharge pipe from the combined filter/aerator a few millimeters below the water surface. Because of the flow of circulating water, a lot of atmospheric oxygen above the surface will be transported to the deeper tank regions.

The Importance of Water Plants in an Aquarium

Plants fulfill numerous functions in an aquarium: they serve as spawning medium and also as protection for many fish species. To a lesser degree, they are also a menu item for some fish. Plants remove large amounts of excess nutrients from the aquarium water, which they then utilize for their own growth. This way, plants also contribute to the cleanliness of the water; however, the single most important function of water plants in an aquarium is the production of oxygen by means of photosynthesis. But green plants do not produce oxygen continuously. Plants will produce an excess of oxygen only during daylight hours or under sufficient artificial lighting. Therefore, you should leave the aquarium lights on for 12 to 14 hours every day. At night, the plants will use up some of the oxygen produced during the day for themselves; the remainder is then available for the respiration of the fish. This way, there is sufficient oxygen available to the fish at night, since most of them are resting and less active, and therefore require significantly less oxygen than during the day.

Buying Water Plants

Before buying, you need to plan in precise detail just how many plants and what species you require for the initial setup of your tank. Keep in mind that the plants available from your aquarium shop are invariably young specimens that tend to grow in the aquarium and subsequently will take up more space and water volume than they do at the outset. Consequently, do not put too many plants into the aquarium; otherwise, they will impede each other's growth and the development of new leaves and branches. Moreover, once acclimatized and well-established, many plant species will send out an abundance of runners.

For most aquariums, it's recommended to place relatively tall-growing, compact species along the back of the tank, and slightly smaller, less massive plants in the central part of the tank. The foreground is either left open, or planted densely with short (2 to 3¼ inch [5 to 8 cm tall]) plants, which will eventually grow together to form a lawn-like cover. Only up to 25–30 percent of the tank's water surface should eventually be covered by floating plants, so that there is always sufficient light penetrating to the lower tank regions.

Be Alert When Buying Water Plants

Once in the aquarium shop, select only plants that appear robust and have sufficient leaves. The leaves must not be yellowish, torn, or chewed on by snails. Moreover, the plants must be free of algae. Examining the roots is very important; except for plant cuttings, the roots must always be strong and well-developed. There should not be any patches of decay or any foul odor present. Many water plants are sold in tiny plastic pots. After the purchase, don't hesitate to remove each plant cautiously and inspect the roots.

The Correct Transport Method

Water plants can be categorized into submersed-growing species and those growing terrestrially.

When planting, make sure to trim excessive root growth first. That has a stimulating effect on the subsequent development of the plant.

Submersed species grow exclusively under water, while terrestrial forms often exhibit a phase where part of the plant emerges above the surface. There are also types of plants that thrive exclusively in very damp terrestrial areas. In order to avoid damage to your newly acquired plants on your way home, you should always transport submersed species (such as water weed, fanwort, and hornwort) in a plastic bag filled with water.

Species that are *littoral*, or where some of the leaves emerge above the surface (e.g., Sword-plants, Cryptocorynes, and Arrowhead [*Sagittaria*]), are more robust. For these, a closed plastic bag without water is sufficient. During the cold winter months, the plastic carrying bag should be wrapped in several layers of newspapers as insulation to protect against frost damage.

Quarantine Before Planting

Newly acquired water plants must first be placed in a small plastic pan or dish filled with lukewarm water, with one of the commercially available anti-aquatic snail substances added to the water. These substances also eradicate undesirable freshwater polyps (Hydra). Subsequently, place this pan in a bright room with an air temperature of at least 64°F (18°C) for two weeks. In the event snails or their eggs were hidden among the leaves, they will be destroyed during that period. Before adding the plants to the aquarium, rinse them off briefly under running water and make a final check of the roots. If they are long, trim all particularly long roots back to a length of about 1¼ to 1¾ inches (about 35 to 40 mm). This does not harm the plants; instead, water plants with shorter roots will become anchored in the substrate more quickly and develop better and stronger.

Magnificent Plant Growth— and How to Achieve It

TIPS FROM AN
AQUARIUM EXPERT
Axel Gutjahr

MAGNIFICENT COLORS: Apart from plants in many shades of green, there are also plant species which are yellowish, wine-red, and violet-red. By skillfully combining them you can achieve spectacular color contrasts in your aquarium.

DIVERSITY OF FORMS: The appearance of water plants is also captivating because of their different growth and leaf shapes and patterns. For instance, you can arrange large-leaf types next to those with small leaves, or plants with elongated leaves next to those with round leaves.

DELICATE CLUSTERS: Water plant species with delicate leaves, such as Water Milfoil (*Myriophyllum*), are aesthetically not very effective as solitary specimens. Therefore, plants like this are best cultivated in dense clusters.

BARE STEMS: With insufficient lighting, some species (e.g. giant *Hygrophila [H.corymbosa]*) lose their leaves along the lower sections of the stem. Plants like this should be pulled out of the substrate and the bare section cut off. Replant the upper part in the substrate, where the plant will develop new roots relatively quickly.

Water Plant Portraits

With variable leaf colors and shapes, water plants contribute significantly to the aesthetic appeal of an aquarium. The plant portraits here will introduce to you some particularly popular and easy-to-care-for aquarium plants.

Dwarf Anubias *(Anubias barteri* var. *nana).* Robust species from West Africa. Should be attached to rocks or tree roots using fishing line. Important for rhizomes to remain above substrate when being planted.

Crinkled Aponogeton *(Aponogeton crispus).* Asian water plant with leaves up to 20 in (50 cm) long. Ideally suited for esthetically structuring the background of an aquarium.

Fanwort *(Cabomba caroliniana).* Rather fine-feathered plant. Most effective when several stems are planted together as individual bunches.

Water Sprite *(Ceratopteris thalictroides).*
This is a fern that belongs to the Brake family (Pteridaceae), which is distributed from Southeast Asia to Australia. It grows to a height of 16 in (40 cm), but its leaves break off easily. Will grow well, even under medium light intensity. Can also be kept as a floating plant on the water surface.

Bronze or Dwarf Cryptocoryne *(Cryptocoryne wendtii).* Small, rather slow-growing species, ideally suited for the foreground in an aquarium.

Javamoss *(Vesicularia dubyana).* Forms dense, dark green cushions, which can be used for hiding or disguising some of the technical support components inside the tank.

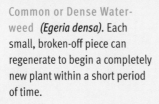

Common or Dense Waterweed *(Egeria densa).* Each small, broken-off piece can regenerate to begin a completely new plant within a short period of time.

American Eelgrass *(Vallisneria americana).* Leaves can reach a total length of more than 39 in (1 m) long and ½ to 1 in (1.25–2.5 cm) wide. Ideally suited for background planting.

An Aquarium Emerges

Finally, you have reached the stage where you will set up your aquarium in a step-by-step manner. You will decorate it, plant it, and then begin its operation. Soon thereafter, fish will provide the life in your underwater world.

Planning Is Half the Work

Make yourself a small sketch of your intended tank layout first, so that later on you don't have to think about where certain plants, various technical components, and decorative items should be placed. Take time to plan out the details and develop several variations of your layout plan, modifying the locations of the respective items and particular plant species. Select the most advantageous version of your sketched proposals. On the basis of this final layout plan, you can check whether the required material and plants are already on hand, or if there is still something that needs to be purchased.

Important Preparations

In order to be sure that your aquarium does not have any leaks, first test it before starting the actual installation work. Take the tank out into the yard or onto a terrace and fill it completely with water. If you do not see water coming out anywhere around the corners or edges of the tank during the following five to six hours, the test is successful.

In the event that you would like to use rock castles, coconut shells, bamboo tubes, or sticks and roots that you collected for decorating your aquarium, everything will need to be appropriately prepared before they can be used in the aquarium.

First, the bamboo roots must be cleaned thoroughly in hot water, using a brush. Thereafter, they should be placed into a tub with clean water for at least 7 to 10 days, with the water renewed every day. This treatment will release certain substances (e.g., large amounts of tannic acid) still present in the roots. Furthermore, the roots will soak up water, which then reduces their initial buoyancy so they will not float to the surface once they have been placed inside the aquarium. This process can be accelerated by weighing down the roots with large rocks to counteract their initial buoyancy.

Setting Up the Aquarium

The first step is to position the aquarium on a stable piece of furniture or (preferably) on a specially designed aquarium cabinet. Fit the plastic backdrop into the tank, or, alternatively, attach the plastic sheet with the printed underwater landscape to the outside of the back panel of the tank. Next, install the (bottom) heater and the intake and discharge pipes of the outside filter. Connect the pipes to the filter via hoses supplied with the filter kit. With an internal filter, you proceed in the same way, preferably placing the unit in one of the corners at the back of the tank. Such a filter can later be camouflaged by strategically positioning large plants in front of it.

Substrate and Decoration

The substrate must be thoroughly washed under running water before it can be placed into the aquarium. Washing is best done in a bucket and needs to be continued until the water clears and all the substrate material has settled at the bottom of the bucket. Distribute the substrate along the bottom of the aquarium in a layer about 1 to 1½ inches (3 to 4 cm) thick. While doing that, make one or two terrace-like elevations in the back of the tank. Shaping these terraces is easy if the substrate is still wet from being washed; however, so that they do not collapse later on, they must be stabilized along their front edges with medium-sized round rocks. With the substrate in place, distribute decorative items throughout the tank. Use only enough decoration to enhance the appeal of your aquarium, combining decorations and plants in a harmonious way. Place coconut shells, rock structures, and bamboo tubes so that their openings point slightly to one side or straight to the front so you can watch your fish swim in and out of these hiding places.

Fill the Tank and Introduce the Plants

Before filling the tank with water, put several layers of newspaper or strong wrapping paper over the entire substrate and place a bowl on top of the paper. Pour the water into the bowl until it flows over and onto the paper. This minimizes stirring up the particles of the substrate, keeping the water clear. Ideally, you should use water at room temperature that has been left standing in one or more containers for two or three days. Continue filling the tank until it is 80 to 90 percent full.

After you have removed the paper and retrieved the bowl from the bottom of the tank, you can start planting. With a thin wooden stick or simply with your index finger, make holes in the substrate. Place the plants into these holes for the length of the (bare) stem, or to a position just above the

---

Close to Nature: How to Do It

If possible, avoid positioning rocks and plants in strict geometrical shapes, such as circles, squares, or absolutely straight lines. Such arrangements always look unnatural. Rock structures must also be realistic and without turrets or other unnatural peaks, because these would inevitably look unnatural and artificial.

---

start of the first leaf. Then gently compact the substrate around each plant until all plants are securely positioned. Now you can fill the tank to a level about ¾ inch (2 cm) below the upper edge of the glass. Finally, place the aquarium light unit on top of the tank and install the lights. Thereafter, start up the aquarium equipment.

Before introducing fish into your new aquarium, the filled and operational tank must undergo a three-week conditioning phase for the water to become properly conditioned and the plants to anchor their roots in the substrate and start growing. At that point, photosynthesis takes place—the production of oxygen by the plants is at full speed.

1ST STEP: First place the aquarium on a stable piece of furniture or on a dedicated aquarium stand or cabinet. Then, install the heaters as well as the intake and discharge pipes of the outside filter, and affix the plastic back wall. Next, connect the pipes via the flexible hoses to the filter.

2ND STEP: Distribute the well-washed substrate along the aquarium bottom. If desired, you can landscape some terrace-like elevations with the substrate. After that, distribute the remaining decorative items throughout the tank and fill it to the 90 percent level.

3RD STEP: Upon completion of planting, fill up the tank completely and start up the equipment. You will still have to wait for three weeks before you can introduce any fish. This period is required to condition the tap water into proper aquarium water.

Habitats of Tropical and Subtropical Fish Species

Some years ago, cold-water fish were still commonly kept in aquariums; however, now species from tropical and subtropical regions are almost exclusively the inhabitants of home aquariums. In their native countries and continents, these species live in very diverse types of aquatic habitats: from large lakes and rivers, to swamps, rice paddies, small jungle streams and ponds, all the way down to ditches and small waterholes that dry out completely during certain times of the year. Some species even live in brackish water, a mixture of seawater and freshwater. The table below provides a review of fish species that are characteristic for particular geographical regions.

ORIGIN	FAMILY/ORDER	EXAMPLES
South America	Cichlids Tetras Catfish Killifish	Angelfish (Pterophyllum scalare) Cardinal Tetra (Paracheirodon axelrodi) Leopard Corydoras (Corydoras julii) Argentine Pearl Fish (Austrolebias bellottii)
Central America & Caribbean	Liverbearers Splitfins Cichlids Catfish	Common Platy (Xiphophorus maculatus) Butterfly Splitfin (Ameca splendens) Firemouth Cichlid (Thorichthys meeki) Royal Farlowella (Sturisoma panamense)
Africa	Catfish Killifish Tetras Cichlids	Large-spot Catfish (Synodontis ocellifer) Lyretail Killifish (Aphyosemion australe) Congo Tetra (Phenacogrammus interruptus) Jewel Cichlid (Hemichromis lifalili)
Southeast Asia	Barbs Badis Killifish Labyrinth fish	Tiger Barb (Puntius tetrazona) Badis (Badis badis) Ceylon Killifish (Aplocheilus dayi) Paradise Fish (Macropodus opercularis)
Australia, Oceania	Rainbow fish Blue-eyes Gobies	Red Rainbow Fish (Glossolepis incisus) Forktail Blue-eye (Pseudomugil furcatus) Desert Goby (Chlamydogobius eremius)

Commercially Bred or Wild-caught?

Fish available from aquarium shops or specialist pet shops are either wild-caught—that is, they came directly from their original habitats—or they have been commercially bred. Far more common than wild-caught fish are those that have been commercially bred, either in local or overseas tropical fish hatcheries. Nowadays, many species (e.g., neon tetras and guppies) are being bred in large fish hatcheries in Southeast Asia and Africa, from which they are air-freighted to Europe and North America. Of course, these are not imported fish in the traditional sense, but indeed they are captive-bred, hatchery fish.

Peculiarities of Commercially Bred Fish

In contrast to wild-caught fish, commercially bred ones often have significantly brighter colors and larger fins. These fish have been genetically modified over generations through intensive breeding, and during this process breeders have modified particular species according to their own imagination, or in response to customer demand. For instance, coral-red platys are substantially easier to sell than those with natural coloration, because of many customers' preference for more intense shades of red.

Similarly, long-finned fish are currently very popular; for instance, rosy barbs, cardinal tetras, and black widows with veil-like, enlarged fins are often more commonly sold than those with normal fins. An extreme example here is that of male Siamese fighting fish (*Betta splendens*), which are also referred to

as veiled fighting fish. When a male of this type spreads its fins to their maximum extent, it is an extremely imposing sight. However, under natural environmental conditions, such a fish is not likely to survive; the size of the fins would be an impediment to a quick escape, and the fish would become an easy victim for a predator. There is, of course, always a price to be paid for selectively breeding for bright colors and modified fins: these fish usually remain an inch or more smaller than comparable wild-caught specimens. Yet, these specially-bred varieties have the advantage that they are more tolerant to water changes than wild-caught fish.

More and more colorful commercially bred fish inhabit home aquariums.

Senses and Anatomy

Gills

Gills are the respiratory organs of fish. They are protected against physical damage by a gill cover.

Eyes

Fish have excellent vision through the rigid lenses of their eyes, used principally for close-up vision. Focal adjustments are made by means of muscles that pull the lens toward the retina.

Barbels

Barbels are fleshy, thread-like appendages on the mouth of a fish, equipped with vast numbers of sensory and taste cells. Generally, only fish that forage along the bottom or actually dig in the substrate in search of food have barbels.

Fins

Fins are the locomotion devices of fish, used for swimming forward as well as in reverse. Fins also serve to stabilize a fish, so that the body does not tip over to one side.

Lateral line

The lateral line starts at the head and ends in the tail. It serves to detect pressure waves and vibrations in the water.

Scales

The body of (most) fish is covered with scales, much like a protective shield. The scales are covered by mucus, which reduces frictional resistance while swimming.

How Many Fish Can My Tank Handle?

Many beginning aquarists make the mistake of keeping too many fish in the aquarium, while at the same time not having sufficient plants in it. With a stocking density that is too high, most fish suffer permanent stress. This in turn leads to a general weakening of the immune system, and the fish become more susceptible to diseases. Fish under stress do not grow well and usually never show their full color potential. In extreme cases, there can even be behavioral disturbances. In order to counteract this right from the start, calculate the suitable specimen density for your tank—the tank's carrying capacity.

Stocking Density

In a well-aerated and adequately planted aquarium, at least ¾–1 gal (about 2–4 l) of water should be available per inch (2.54 cm) of fish length. As an example, for a 26.5 gal (100-l) tank intended to be stocked with 2 inch (5 cm)-long Black Widow Tetras *(Gymnocorymbus ternetzi)*, we use the following calculation:

From 26.5 gal (100 l) total volume, we subtract 4.6 gal (17.5 l) for substrate, decoration, and equipment (about 17–20 percent of the total volume) = 21.9 gal (82.5 l) water volume; 21.9 gal volume / 1 gal of water per inch of fish length = 55 inches of total fish length/ 1 inch length per specimen = 11 Black Widow Tetras with a length not exceeding one inch (2.54 cm).

Apart from the water volume, the length and width of the aquarium are also of significance for the number of fish that can be kept there. The ratio of length to width to body length of the fish should be approximately 10:5:1 for fast-swimming species (e.g., Rosy Barbs [*Puntius conchonius*]) . For less active species—for instance Siamese Fighting Fish (*Betta splendens*)—a ratio of 8:4:1 is sufficient.

Black Widow Tetras, a South American species, are most contented in groups of at least six to eight specimens.

Composition of the Fish Population in Your Tank

An aquarium is particularly attractive when all areas of the tank are alive with activity. Therefore, for the composition of your tank you should select fish that live along the bottom, in the middle water layers, and some that inhabit the space just below the water surface.

Be Careful with Aggressive Species

Make sure that you select only peaceful species for your aquarium. Aggressive species, such as Lifalili Jewel Cichlids, will introduce an element of restlessness and anxiety. Such "fish ruffians" will attack the other inhabitants with biting or headbutting. The victims of such attacks then tend to go into more or less permanent hiding.

Avoid Mistakes

Beginners often make the mistake of not keeping their fish in a species-correct manner (e.g., keeping those species in pairs that should really be kept in a small group). In the "Expert Tip" on this page you can read about how to keep certain fish. Some species are incompatible with each other: for instance, the very popular Sumatra barbs should not be kept together with angelfish or labyrinth fish. In the latter two, the pelvic fins are modified into large threads and the perpetually hungry Sumatra barbs have a tendency to completely nibble off these threads, thinking that they are worms. For the affected victims, this will cause pain and a lot of stress. Another example: keeping closely related species, such as sword tails and platys, together in the same tank, can lead to undesirable crossbreeding (hybridization).

Social Organizations of Fish

TIPS FROM AN
AQUARIUM EXPERT
Axel Gutjahr

Important forms of association among fish are:

SCHOOL: You should keep nearly all barbs, tetras, live-bearing tooth-carps, and *Corydoras* catfish in groups (schools) of at least six to eight specimens.

HAREM: The majority of South American *Corydoras* catfish are most contented if one male is kept together with two to four females. Moreover, each female should have at least one cave available to her as a hiding place.

PAIR: Many cichlids prefer to be kept in pairs. Under no circumstances should you add yet another male, because that would lead to physical aggression among the pair.

TERRITORIAL SPECIES: Males of some cichlids, such as the Dwarf Mouthbrooder (*Pseudocrenilabrus multicolor*) or those of the Dwarf Gourami (*Colisa lalia*), occupy a small territory where they will tolerate only females that are ready to spawn. Therefore, sufficient hiding places must be available for females not yet ready to spawn.

Peocilia velifera
Sailfin Molly

Family: Sailfin Mollies belong to the live-bearing tooth-carps (*livebearers*); females can reach a total length of 7 in (18 cm), males 6 in (15 cm). **Origin:** Mexican peninsula of Yucatan, where they occur primarily in coastal waters. **Aquarium maintenance:** In groups with an excess of females; these agile fish prefer to inhabit the middle regions of the water tank. They feed on small live food, dried foods, and plant/vegetable materials. **pH:** 7.5 to 8.5. **Temperature:** 75 to 82°F (24 to 20°C). **Water hardness:** 20 to 30 dGH.

Poecilia reticulata
Guppy

Family: Live-bearing tooth-carps (*livebearers*): The anal fin in males has become modified into a copulatory organ (*gonopodium*). Females are silvery to faint beige; up to 2¼ in (5.5 cm). The smaller, colorful males reach a total length of less than 1 inch (2 cm). Many color varieties, including those with conspicuous fin enlargements, are commonly available in the aquarium trade. **Origin:** Northern South America and some Caribbean Islands. **Aquarium maintenance:** In groups, with an excess of females. Requires lots of swimming space. **Food requirements:** Same as Sailfin Molly. **pH:** 7.2 to 8.0. **Temperature:** 75 to 82°F (24 to 28°C); **Water hardness:** 15 to 25 dGH.

Xiphophorus helleri
Swordtail

Family: Live-bearing tooth-carps (*livebearers*). Females up to 6 in (15 cm), males usually smaller at 4 in (10 cm), measured without the swordlike extension of the tail fin. There are numerous commercially bred color and fin varieties. **Origin:** Central America. **Aquarium maintenance:** Keep in groups with an excess of females. Swordtails tend to frequent the central and upper water layers. **Food requirements:** Same as for Sailfin Mollies. **pH:** 7.0 to 8.0. **Temperature:** 72 to 79°F (22 to 26°C). **Water hardness:** 20 to 30 dGH.

Pterophyllum scalare
Angelfish

Family: Cichlids. Both sexes reach up to 6 in (15 cm) total length; mature males generally have a bulging forehead. Also bred commercially as different color varieties and with enlarged fins. **Origin:** Amazon River, including tributaries from Peru to Ecuador. **Aquarium maintenance:** In pairs. Very peaceful species that does not damage plants or dig in substrate. **Food requirements:** Feeds on live and dried foods, but particle size must not be too small. **pH:** 6.3 to 7.5. **Temperature:** 75 to 82°F (24 to 28°C). **Water Hardness:** 5 to 15 dGH.

Pelvicachromis pulcher
Dwarf Rainbow Cichlid or "Kribensis"

Family: Cichlids. Males—6 in (15 cm) total length—slightly paler than females, dorsal and anal fins drawn out to a point. Females smaller than males, less than 1 in (2.54 cm), with crimson-colored abdomen during the breeding period. **Origin:** Nigeria; common in Niger-Delta. **Aquarium maintenance:** In pairs. Peaceful species that needs a tank with caves. Active in lower and middle areas of tank. **Food requirements:** Will accept nearly all live, frozen, and dried foods. **pH:** 6.5 to 7.0. **Temperature:** 75 to 79°F (24 to 26°C). **Water hardness:** 5 to 15 dGH.

Apistogramma borellii
Borelli's Dwarf Cichlid

Family: Cichlids. The 2.4 in (6 cm) long male is more colorful than the female and it has larger fins. Maximum size of the female is 1¼ in (3 cm). **Origin:** Flowing waters of southern Brazil and northern Argentina. **Aquarium maintenance:** In pairs or one male and two females. Peaceful and compatible with other community tank fish. Should be given caves and leaves scattered over the substrate. Inhabits areas close to the bottom of the tank. **Food requirements:** Should be given water fleas (*Daphnia*) and Cyclops frequently. **pH:** 6.0 to 6.5. Temperature: 77–82°F (25–28°C). **Water hardness:** 5 to 15 dGH.

Gymnocorymbus ternetzi
Black Widow Tetra

Family: Tetras. Easily 2 in (5 cm) long. Sexes difficult to distinguish. Males slightly more slender and marginally smaller. **Origin:** Various waters in Brazil, Bolivia, and Paraguay. **Aquarium maintenance:** In a school of at least six specimens. Usually swims calmly in the middle water layers; very peaceful. **Food requirements:** Prefers live flies struggling on the water surface; will readily accept all live and artificial foods. **pH:** 6.0 to 7.5. **Temperature:** 72 to 79°F (22 to 26°C). **Water hardness:** 5 to 15 dGH.

Hyphessobrycon flammeus
Flame Tetra

Family: Tetras. Maximum length to 1¾ in (4.5 cm). Abdominal and anal fins of the smaller and slenderer male have a black edge. **Origin:** Inhabits swamps and slow-flowing waters in the vicinity of Rio de Janeiro (Brazil). **Aquarium maintenance:** School of at least 10 specimens. **Food requirements:** Accepts nearly all types of food, but has a preference for live black mosquito larvae. **pH:** 6.5 to 7.0. **Temperature:** 72 to 81°F (22 to 27°C). **Water hardness:** 5 to 15 dGH.

Danio rerio
Zebrafish

Family: Minnows (carp relatives). The 2¼ in (6 cm) long male is marginally smaller than the female and has more intense colors, but the female can be equally as attractive. **Origin:** Northern India. **Aquarium maintenance:** Group of at least six specimens. There are also purpose-bred varieties with veil-like fins. Very agile and peaceful fish. **Food requirements:** Similar to those listed for Flame Tetra. **pH:** 6.5 to 7.5. **Temperature:** 64 to 75°F (18 to 24°C). **Water hardness:** 5 to 15 dGH.

Puntius conchonius
Rosy Barb

Family: Minnows (carp-like fish). The 2¾ in (7 cm) long male is marginally smaller and more intensely colored than the female. The similarly attractive female is reddish-green. **Origin:** Northern India. **Aquarium maintenance:** Group of at least six specimens. Agile, peaceful fish; commercially bred, veil-finned varieties are also available. **Food requirements:** An undemanding species that will accept nearly all types of fish food. **pH:** 6.5 to 7.5. **Temperature:** 64 to 75°F (18 to 24°C). **Water hardness:** 5 to 15 dGH.

Colisa lalia
Dwarf Gourami

Family: Labyrinth fish. Males grow to a maximum length of 2¼ in (6 cm); with dorsal and anal fins extended to a point, they are far more colorful than the smaller female. **Origin:** India. **Aquarium maintenance:** In groups of one male with two to three females. **Food requirements:** Will accept live, frozen, and plant/vegetable foods. Should not be kept together with very active fish. Apart from gill respiration, this fish will also pick up atmospheric oxygen at the surface. **pH:** 6.5 to 7.5. **Temperature:** 72 to 82°F (22 to 28°C). **Water hardness:** 5 to 20 dGH.

Trichogaster trichopterus
Blue Gourami

Family: Labyrinth fish. Males up to 4¾ in (12 cm) long with an extended, pointed dorsal fin. Females slightly smaller and with a more rounded abdominal section. **Origin:** Widely distributed through Southeast Asia. **Aquarium maintenance:** One male with two to three females. Dense plant thickets required as retreat areas for females. **Food requirements:** Similar to those listed for Dwarf Gourami. Will also pick up atmospheric oxygen at the surface. **pH:** 6.0 to 8.0. **Temperature:** 72 to 82°F (22 to 28°C). **Water hardness:** 5 to 20 dGH.

Corydoras aeneus
Bronze Corydoras

Family: Armored Catfish. To 2¾ in (7 cm). Females are slightly larger and somewhat more stout-bodied. **Origin:** Widely distributed throughout South America. **Aquarium maintenance:** In schools of at least eight specimens. Peaceful bottom fish that can utilize atmospheric oxygen by means of adsorption in the digestive tract. **Food requirements:** Will feed on small particles of live, frozen, or artificial fish foods. These fish actively scour the bottom of the tank for food, and consequently do not use sharp-edged gravel as substrate that could cause injuries to the catfish. **pH:** 6.5 to 7.5. **Temperature:** 72 to 79°F (22 to 26°C). **Water hardness:** 5 to 20 dGH.

Ancistrus dolichopterus
Bushymouth Catfish

Family: Suckermouth Armored Catfish. Both sexes grow to a maximum length of 5½ in (14 cm). Males have substantial "beard" around mouth and on forehead, which actually consists of tentacle-like skin outgrowths. **Origin:** Amazon region. **Aquarium maintenance:** In pairs or one male with two to three females. Male establishes and maintains a territory, driving off all competitors, but very peaceful toward other species in a community tank. **Food requirements:** Feeds extensively on plant material. **pH:** 5.8 to 7.5. **Temperature:** 72 to 82°F (22 to 28°C). **Water hardness:** 5 to 20 dGH.

Melanotaenia maccullochi
Dwarf Rainbowfish

Family: Rainbowfish. Both sexes grow up to 2¾ in (7 cm) long, but the male is more slender and has enhanced colors. **Origin:** Southern Papua-New Guinea to northeastern Australia. **Aquarium maintenance:** In groups of at least six specimens. Very active swimmers; mainly in the middle water levels in an aquarium. Requires substantial, weekly water change (about 25% of tank volume). **Food requirements:** Preference for small live food, but will accept most types of aquarium fish food with a small particle size. **pH:** 6.0 to 7.5. **Temperature:** 75 to 86°F (24 to 30°C). **Water hardness:** 20 to 30 dGH.

Marosatherina ladigesi
Celebes Rainbowfish

Family: Sailfin Silversides. Maximum length 2¾ in (7 cm); males may be slightly larger, with dorsal and anal fins extensively enlarged and more colorful than females. **Origin:** Celebes (formerly Sulawesi), Indonesia. **Aquarium maintenance:** In groups of at least eight specimens. Very active swimmers. Comprehensive weekly water change required. **Food requirements:** Will take nearly all types of aquarium fish food, including some plant matter. **pH:** 7.0. **Temperature:** 72 to 81°F (22 to 27°C). **Water hardness:** 20 to 25 dGH.

Aplocheilus lineatus
Striped Panchax

Family: Egg-laying tooth-carps. Maximum length 4¾ in (12 cm). Females with dark spot in the dorsal fin; only marginally smaller than males and not as colorful. **Origin:** Indian Subcontinent. **Aquarium maintenance:** In pairs or in groups with an excess of females. Strong orientation to the surface; the tank should have a partial cover of floating water plants. **Food requirements:** Will accept live, frozen, and artificial fish foods, with a preference for large food items. **pH:** 6.0 to 7.0. **Temperature:** 72 to 81°F (22 to 27°C). **Water hardness:** 5 to 20 dGH.

Fundulopanchax gardneri
Steel-blue Killifish

Family: Egg-laying tooth-carps. Very colorful males reach a maximum size of 3¼ in (8 cm); the light brown females are only marginally smaller. **Origin:** Southeastern Nigeria to southwestern Cameroon. **Aquarium maintenance:** Should be kept in groups, with an excess of females. Hierarchical fighting among males. Prefers middle water regions and the proximity of the bottom. **Food requirements:** Similar to those of the Striped Panchax. **pH:** 6.0 to 6.5. **Temperature:** 71 to 77°F (22 to 25°C). **Water hardness:** 5 to 15 dGH.

Snails, Shrimps, and African Clawed Frogs

Apart from fish, you can also keep various species of water snails, freshwater shrimp, and African Clawed Frogs in your aquarium.

Snails

Water snails are often praised as regular aquarium cleaners that will keep an aquarium totally free of algae. Unfortunately, the reality is often quite different. Most snails feed on green algae only if algal growth in the aquarium is not too extensive or too lush. However, if a regular green algae explosion ever does happen in your aquarium, snails will make little, if any, difference. Apart from green algae, snails also like to feed on dead leaves of water plants and on leftover food particles; however, fish eggs are indeed a real delicacy for snails. Aquatic snails usually multiply very rapidly. In such an event the favorite food of snails available in the aquarium may become scarce, and when that happens, snails will not hesitate to feed on delicate water plants. They will also chew characteristic round holes into the leaves of tougher water plants. Therefore, you will need to closely monitor the development of the snail population in your aquarium.

Shrimp

Small, peaceful fish can readily be kept together with some freshwater shrimp; yet large fish usually pursue them as food. Various freshwater shrimp species, some of them quite attractive, are frequently available from the aquarium trade. It is also alleged that freshwater shrimp are very good algae removers, but that too is only partially correct; freshwater shrimp may be able to remove them as long as the growth of filamentous, bearded, and red/brown algae is only moderate. Yet, in most cases, three or four shrimp will be insufficient to handle a real algal problem. For that you will require at least 30 to 40 shrimp.

Frogs

African Clawed Frogs, which can reach a size of up to ½ inch (4 cm) can also be kept in a community aquarium together with small peaceful fish species such as live-bearing tooth-carps. For these amphibians to be content in the aquarium, they need to be given numerous hiding places.

You should only keep shrimp together with small, very peaceful fish.

What Should I Do When My Fish Breed?

When fish reproduce in a community aquarium, it is always a sign that the environmental conditions are indeed suitable for them. Especially live-bearing tooth-carps (livebearers) and cichlids often surprise aquarium hobbyists when there is suddenly a school of tiny fish larvae in their aquarium.

Surprise Blessing of Fish Offspring

As immense as the initial joy over the newly discovered baby fish progeny may be, it can quickly develop into a problem. As soon as the majority of these youngsters—it can be several hundred if they are cichlids—have started to grow, space in the aquarium can become extremely tight. Should this happen, and there is no other tank available as a fish nursery, the biological balance in the aquarium will be severely disrupted. But even if a fish-rearing tank is available, you need to make sure that there is someone who will take these little fish off your hands once they have grown. Certainly some of the aquarium shops in your area are normally willing to take 30 or 40 young cichlids off your hands—but it is more prudent to check on this beforehand. On the other hand, 150 to 200 young fish may be too many even for a retail shop. So what to do with all the excess fish? The only thing left to do is to find a tropical fish wholesaler in your area with the hope that he will be able to take the entire brood off your hands.

Be Prudent—Take Precautions Early

It is best not to let matters get that far. Right from the start, you can avoid the surprise of suddenly finding several hundred baby fish in your tank. Simply purchase a few Redchin Panchax (*Epiplatys dageti*), Bleeding Heart Tetras (*Hyphessobrycon erythrostigma*), or some African Butterfly Fish (*Pantodon buchholzi*) for your tank, and they will take care of any emerging problems of this nature; they are all aggressive predators of the baby fish. This measure does not mean that you do not have a heart for animals. Quite to the contrary—eating and being eaten are completely natural behaviors that occur every day in nature and contribute to the maintenance of all animal species. Keeping species in your tank that will feed on excess juvenile fish contributes to maintaining your tank's biological balance, and so protects you against many problems of this nature.

Cichlids will breed readily, even in a community tank. Here we have a Jewel Cichlid female with her progeny.

Selecting and Purchasing Fish

Take your time when buying fish for your aquarium. First, take a good look at the specimens in the tanks of the aquarium or pet shop. The fish there must give an impression of being healthy and appear agile. You must not buy specimens with open sores or tumors, deformed backbones, or white spots on body or fins. Similarly, cloudy eyes and badly torn or missing fins should discourage you from a purchase. Do not select any fish from a tank where there are dead specimens on the bottom. Colored water (e.g., clear yellowish, greenish, or bluish tinge) in any of the shop's tanks is invariably due to medication in the water; not exactly a good recommendation. On the other hand, if the fish in a dealer's tank are not as colorful as you have seen them in photographs, this not a reason for rejecting them. Most fish for sale are usually juveniles that have not yet reached the full color potential of adults. Furthermore, the fish in a shop's sale display tanks are under considerable stress, which causes a temporary decline in color intensity.

Transporting Fish

Taking your newly purchased fish home requires several plastic transport bags, because each bag should contain only specimens from the same tank in the shop. If you have a long way to go home, carry the bags in a foam box with a tightly fitting lid. This way the water temperature remains constant and the darkness reduces stress on the fish. As an alternative to a foam box, you can also wrap the plastic bags in several layers of newspaper.

Temperature Adjustment

In the event that the water temperature in the plastic transport bags and in your home aquarium are not the same, the temperature in the bags will need to be adjusted to that of your tank. For that purpose you must float the bags on the aquarium surface for 30 to 60 minutes so that the temperature in the bags changes gradually to that of the tank. Once the temperature has been equalized, the fish can be permitted to swim into their new surroundings.

1 Plastic bags are ideally suited for transporting newly purchased fish.

2 Before releasing the fish into the aquarium, the water temperature must be carefully adjusted.

Fish Food in Review

A wide range of aquarium fish food is available from aquarium and pet shops. In addition, you can also catch your own in fish-free ponds, ditches surrounding pastures and fields, and from open rainwater barrels (more about that on page 44).

Major Types of Fish Food

Live food is closest to the normal fish diet in nature. In addition, it stimulates the innate prey and hunting behavior of fish. A distinct disadvantage of live food is the fact that with it disease pathogens can easily be introduced into your aquarium. Moreover, many types of live food (e.g., water fleas) are not available throughout the year.

Frozen food is fresh frozen live food, which has a high nutritional value. The production method of such food usually kills off disease pathogens.

Dried foods (such as dried *Daphnia* or mosquito larvae) have less nutritional value than live or frozen foods; however, commercially produced artificial (dried) foods are available in stores vacuum-packed, their nutritional value enhanced with vitamins and trace elements. Keep in mind that such foods may well be high in nutritional value, but this quality is lost rapidly once a package is opened. Therefore, buy small packages only and feed the contents to your fish quickly—BUT without over-feeding your fish.

Vegetable (plant) matter is an important dietary component in the food of many species (e.g., live-bearing tooth-carps and catfish). For that reason, there should be at least a few algae-covered rocks in the aquarium. In addition, you can offer finely chopped lettuce or spinach to livebearers. Catfish, especially when they are large, also accept chopped, fresh potatoes, kohlrabi, and zucchini slices. All leftover (uneaten) food pieces MUST be removed from the aquarium not later than six hours after the feeding, so that they cannot decompose and adversely affect the water quality.

When you buy dried foods, make sure that these are of the highest quality. In particular, make sure that they contain many additional vitamins.

43

Collecting Your Own Live Fish Food

Those little worm-like creatures that you can find wiggling near the surface of the water of rainbarrels and small puddles are usually the larvae and pupae of mosquitoes, generally referred to as black mosquito larvae. They are rich in protein and also contain substances that stimulate many fish into breeding. One of the closest relatives of black mosquito larvae, red mosquito larvae, are often found in huge numbers in standing outdoor waters. The reddish coloration of their bodies is due to an above-average hemoglobin content, which has also led to the name "blood worms."

Clear, still forest waters are the preferred habitats for the white or glass mosquito larvae. These thrive throughout the year and are among the most important food components during the winter months. Reddish or brownish water fleas (*Daphnia*) are the classical food animals for aquarium fish. Although water fleas—which belong to the group (order Cladocera) of small crustaceans—have low caloric value, they should be fed periodically to your fish. The digestive tract of these tiny crustaceans always contains small green algae particles that have important vitamins. When digesting water fleas, fish will also absorb many of these vitamins. Another group of small crustaceans are grayish to greenish copepods (subclass Copepoda; various species), characterized by a high nutritional value; they are usually very eagerly eaten by many small fish. However, caution is advised when feeding your fish live food organisms because of an inherent danger of introducing fish diseases and parasites into the aquarium.

Also regularly available from the aquarium trade are so-called mud worms, usually referred to as *tubifex*; however, you should feed these only to your fish every 7 to 10 days. Tubifex worms are rich in calories and so they can readily lead to obesity among your fish. Large fish, especially many of the cichlids, should be given, as well as at least occasionally, more substantial food items, such as a few well-washed earthworms, about once a week.

Live food stimulates the natural prey capture and hunting behavior of your fish.

Feeding Correctly the Easy Way

Feeding fish is a lot of fun. But you must not overdo it; too much or the wrong type of food can readily lead to diseases or nutritional deficiencies in fish. In the worst case scenario it can even cause death.

What to Do

What Not to Do

(+) Feed your fish sensibly. Use this general rule: food not completely eaten within two to three minutes is too much.

(+) Offer a diversified diet. Make a feeding plan.

(+) Adult fish should be fed twice a day (in the morning and at night).

(+) Initially, young fish are given food five to six times a day. Later on, reduce feeding frequency and at the same time increase the amount of food given.

(+) Once a week (or three times in two weeks) do not feed at all. Fasting promotes the vitality and health of your fish. Your fish will look for leftover food and help keep your tank clean.

(−) Do not run the filter while feeding is in progress; otherwise, some of the food will be sucked into the filter.

(−) Do not permit artificial, dried, or frozen food remnants to remain in the tank for a prolonged period. The food will decompose and adversely affect water quality.

(−) Specialist feeders such as the African butterfly fish take their food from the surface. These fish will not be able to change their feeding habit because it is an innate type of behavior.

(−) You must never give bread or bread crumbs as substitute food to aquarium fish. Such food can lead to metabolic disorders.

Practical Aquarium Keeping

The be-all and end-all of every aquarium is correct care and maintenance. Here we show you how to keep your tank fully functional, especially for the optimal development of your fish and plants so that you will be able to enjoy your aquarium more with every day gone by.

How to Keep Your Tank Intact

The first weeks of setting up your tank and patiently waiting during the conditioning phase are now behind you. Finally, fish will liven up your aquarium. Every day you discover something new in your aquarium and you thoroughly enjoy the beautiful colors and the interesting behavior of the tank's inhabitants. Fish and plants live together in harmony.

This aesthetically appealing image will be maintained if you carry out certain care and maintenance tasks on a regular basis. It will eliminate occasionally occurring problems immediately. This way your aquarium will not become just a glass box with dirty, moldy-smelling water where water plants have become stunted and pale-looking fish swim listlessly behind algae-covered glass walls.

Yet, even with regular care, more can be less: only perform those maintenance tasks that are required; do not "play around" with your tank during every free minute you have. In many cases, overzealousness can have a detrimental effect on plant growth and on the normal behavior of fish.

It is not uncommon for other family members to want to participate in the care of the aquarium. When this happens, it is critically important to have a complete consensus on all tasks that need to be performed. This way you avoid performing some of these tasks repeatedly and missing others altogether. Children especially often tend to feed the fish too frequently and too much. Understandably, fish feeding can be a lot of fun, but you are not doing the fish any favors. You must explain clearly to the children the negative consequences this has on the health and well-being of the fish, and then keep an eye on this situation. In the long term, it is also advisable to train another person in the care and maintenance routines; they will then be in a position to look after your aquarium effectively if you are gone for any significant length of time.

Care and Maintenance

For an aquarium where a biological balance has been largely established, you need to allocate only about 10 to 15 minutes per day for the required care and maintenance.

Every morning you need to check briefly whether all mechanical components are working properly, that the water is clear, and the fish appear to be healthy. After that you give a moderate feeding. While feeding, you should observe the fish behavior closely: even among apparently healthy fish there can be a sudden change in feeding behavior, which is often the first sign of the onset of a disease. Such fish must then be visually examined for external dis-

ease symptoms and then closely monitored over the following days. Also, during the winter months, make sure to open the room where your aquarium is located to the outside air at least five to 10 minutes every morning. This elevates the oxygen content in the room so that during the day an active gas exchange can take place between the air in the room and the water surface of the aquarium.

Feed your fish in the evening, at least one hour before turning off the tank lights. At that time, you should also check once again all equipment items for normal functioning.

Routine Weekly Maintenance Program

On one day a week you need to dedicate 1 to 1½ hours to your aquarium for maintenance. You should select a particular day for this that fits well into your weekly activity schedule, a day where you can do the more comprehensive weekly aquarium maintenance tasks.

That day you exchange at least 20 percent (about ⅓ of the total volume of smaller tanks) of the aquarium water with fresh water. You can use a hose for siphoning out the water, holding the suction end of the hose about ½ to about 1 inch (1 to 2 cm) above the substrate, but close enough to siphon out debris, decaying plant leaves, and uneaten food particles from the bottom at the same time. The water removed from the aquarium this way is suitable for watering your indoor and

The substrate is easy to clean with a gravel cleaner. This cleaning method is extremely gentle on your aquarium.

outdoor plants. The water used for refilling the tank should have been left standing in a separate container for one to two days before use in a partial water change. You also need to make sure that the temperature difference between the aquarium water and the replacement (fresh) water is not larger than three to four degrees. Beyond that, the pH values must be close to identical.

Before you refill the aquarium, you should clean the inside of all glass sides of algae accumulations, using a sponge or a glass scraper. If algae have also settled on rocks and tank decorations, they can be temporarily taken out of the tank and cleaned separately under running water and using a small brush. If some of the plants have dead leaves, these should be gently pulled off. Plants with bare stems should be pulled out of the substrate, their stems cut back and then planted in the substrate again (see Expert Tip on page 21).

Bunches of java moss and moss cushions with accumulated debris on them should be taken out of the aquarium and repeatedly (but gently) dunked in a bucket of lukewarm water so that the debris particles become dislodged. With a small, round wooden, or some other inert material, rod (or even with your index finger!) poke carefully into the substrate at a number of locations along the entire bottom of the aquarium. This measure serves to loosen up the substrate, so that the water can circulate easier through it. In turn, this prevents the formation of decay within the substrate. In extreme cases, large amounts of hydrogen sulfide will develop within such foul-smelling black patches, resulting in the release of a gas with a "rotten egg" smell that rises to the surface and is highly toxic to fish.

If there has been a large buildup of snails, you will need to remove most of them by hand. The fil-

If your water plants proliferate wildly, they need to be trimmed back, which is easily done with a pair of scissors.

ter needs to be cleaned thoroughly every two to three weeks. This is done by washing the upper, coarse filter layer in lukewarm water until the water remains clear.

Half a Day Every Three Months

About once every three months or so, a major cleaning is required, which is essentially an extension of the daily and weekly care and maintenance routine. Apart from the tasks already described, this includes a thorough cleaning of the filter intake and discharge pipes (including the connecting hoses) of algae that will always grow on and inside of these pipes. This particular cleaning is best done with a special very small pipe cleaner. When attached to a string, the pipe cleaner can then be pulled easily through the hoses, removing any algae present.

The filter tubes can also be cleaned with a household steam pressure cleaner. The interior of coconut half shells, bamboo tubes, roots, and rock caves also need to be thoroughly cleaned. For these tasks you must never use chemicals or abrasive domestic cleaning substances, but always only hot water, possibly with an ample amount of common household salt as an additive. In order to remove any salt remnants, all cleaned objects must subsequently be rinsed off thoroughly under running water before they are returned to the aquarium. You also need to check for any areas of decay or other deterioration on the (palm) leaves scattered over the substrate or on any of the roots. Should this be the case, remove these items immediately and replace them with new ones. As a rule, you will need to thin out some of the water plants. If you remove entire plants, you must also remove their roots from the substrate. If these remain in the substrate, they will inevitably start to decay. Plant care also includes severing runners from the maternal plant. This is important, so that the energy of the maternal plant is directed toward its own growth instead of being invested in developing runners. A thorough, deep loosening-up of the entire substrate is another important task during this quarterly service of your aquarium. During this process, a lot of suspended particles will be stirred up, so that about half of the aquarium water should be replaced.

Major Maintenance of the Aquarium

A major general cleaning, whereby the entire tank is emptied out, followed by a complete restructuring of the tank layout, should only be done when it is absolutely necessary. It can happen that this may become necessary as early as one year after the

During a partial water change, the water in an aquarium is siphoned out directly into a bucket.

Older Aquariums

If you had your aquarium in operation for several years, a major general maintenance service may reveal that the old tank needs to be exchanged for a new one. This may be advisable if you discover severe scratches on the sides of the tank (especially on the inside of the front panel). You must never ignore such scratches, because this signals a potential danger that the water pressure could create so much tension on the glass that it could burst.

initial start up of the aquarium; sometimes this may take three or four years. A decisive criteria is the condition of the substrate. If it contains a lot of accumulated debris and other dirt or shows large, blackish patches of decay that cannot be removed during routine maintenance work, the time may indeed have come for such a relatively comprehensive solution. For that reason, a general cleaning requires proper preparation. First, look for opportunities where you can accommodate the fish and plants on a temporary basis. This can be, for instance, in a large plastic tub, in which the water is amply aerated using a circulating pump, in order to provide at least reasonably tolerable conditions for the fish. Three days prior to the general cleaning service stop all feeding. This way there will be hardly any fecal matter once the fish are in their new home; consequently, there is no additional water pollution that would place a further burden on the already stressed-out fish. Once the tank is completely empty, some of the limestone encrustations that may have become deposited due to evaporation along the upper edges of the tank can easily be removed with acetic or citric acid.

Getting Ready for Winter

Fluorescent tubes must be replaced every six to nine months because their light efficiency will have notably deteriorated by then. If possible, make arrangements for such an exchange to take place in October if you live in the Northern Hemisphere, or in March if you live south of the equator (e.g., most of South America, South Africa, or Australia). This way

your aquarium will go into the winter with the tank lights at their optimum capacity. You should also thin out the water plants again, so that they do not take away any light from each other during the darker months of the year, causing them to deteriorate. If need be, you can also reduce your fish inventory by a few specimens, if the threshold value for specimen density in your tank has been reached or has even exceeded that described on page 32. If you are feeding commercial foods to your fish, and if you are not able to visit your aquarium dealer or a pet shop during the winter, make sure that you have appropriate and sufficient supplies on hand.

Cleaning roots is ideally done using a brush and under running tap water. Scrubbing must be proper and very thorough.

Algae in the Aquarium

There is no aquarium in existence that does not carry at least a few representatives of the estimated 35,000 to 40,000 species of green and blue-green algae. Regular aquarium maintenance, together with the presence of water plants, often prevents excessive algae growth. However, during the summer months there can sometimes be a mass reproduction of green algae because the aquarium may have been exposed for too long to direct sunlight. Do not concentrate solely on the mere eradication of algae, but also, if possible, eliminate the causes for any excessive algal development.

Algae Eradication

In the event that too much sun exposure has been the cause for the algae in your aquarium, you can easily darken the particular window through which the tank receives its sun exposure, using a pull-down shade or simply a curtain. In addition, you will need to withhold nutrients for the rapidly growing green algae and diatoms. Therefore, on a daily basis, siphon out nearly all of the water in the aquarium, and replace it with fresh water. At the same time, remove large algae cushions by hand or use a finely porous sponge. A thin wooden stick or rod is ideally suited for the removal of filamentous green algae that often establish themselves as a delicately threaded web, especially over fine-feathery, bushy water plants. Simply wrap the tips of the algae threads around the wooden stick or rod, and then pull these pests gently away from the water plants and out of the tank.

After a week, you can modify the algae eradication program, starting a treatment using dry barley or wheat straw. This method is harmless to fish and water plants. For every 25 gallons (about 100 liters) of aquarium water, place four handfuls of this straw firmly into an old nylon stocking and tie it off, then place the stocking into the aquarium. As early as a few hours afterwards, the tank water will turn cloudy and yellowish, but the turbidity will progressively disappear, while the yellow coloration usu-

Shrimp like to feed on green algae, but they cannot keep a large aquarium algae-free unless there are at least 30 or more shrimp in such a tank.

Black Mollies (*Poecilia sphenops* var.), from among the live-bearing tooth-carps, are the best algae eaters.

Snails love to graze on algae, but once the algae are gone, snails will then attack water plants.

ally remains. A few days later the first algae patches die off, and you will have to siphon them out of the tank daily and then fill the tank up again with fresh water. Two weeks later, you need to replace the straw inside the bag. In most instances, your tank will be free of visible algae after four or five weeks. At that point you remove the straw-filled stocking and again change 90 percent of the water in the tank with fresh water.

Blue-green Algae – Be Patient!

Blue-green algae are large, interconnected bacteria accumulations of bluish-black to black coloration. They are difficult to deal with in an aquarium, and often you need to be very patient. Apart from frequent water changes, you can really only pull them off the glass and off the substrate—as well as off the aquarium décor—with your hands several times daily. Subsequently, any fragments or small patches of blue-green algae suspended in the water must be siphoned out of the aquarium. It is

not uncommon for such an eradication procedure to take three to four months before there is any success. Unfortunately, there are no other more effective treatment methods. The only advice I can give to any hobbyist struggling with blue-green algae in his aquarium is: you need to be more stubborn and persistent than the blue-green algae, and only then will you come out on top!

Green Water in the Summer

Tiny, suspended green algae can turn aquarium water green during the summer. Cover your tank completely with cardboard for three to five days. Plants and fish can handle this without sustaining any harm, but the suspended algae will not survive. Thereafter, remove the card cover gradually, starting at one corner of the tank; this enables the fish to re-adjust to daylight.

Snail Invasion – What to Do?

Water snails are a frequent topic in discussions among aquarium hobbyists. While some of them absolutely refuse to do without them and deliberately introduce apple snails or Brazilian racing snails into their aquariums, for others they are regular thorns in the side. Often snails are introduced inadvertently into an aquarium via water plants or together with live food. Water snails can quickly develop into a real problem when they start multiplying at a rapid rate. When this happens, aquarium hobbyists look for ways and means to get rid of these pests quickly and effectively.

In the table below, I show you how to proceed against snails, together with the prospects of success with particular methods, so that you are in a position to deal with this problem effectively.

Dealing with Snails

ERADICATION METHOD	APPLICATION AND OUTLOOK FOR SUCCESS
Mechanical eradication: Picking snails off by hand	Regular, manual removal of snails can keep their numbers in check, but total eradication is hardly achievable. Many of the pinhead-sized juveniles remain unseen; moreover, a lot of snail eggs remain on water plants, rocks, and roots, which will quickly give rise to a new generation of snails.
Biological eradication, using bait: Just before turning off the tank lights in the evening, place a small dish with raw carrots or raw meat inside the tank	Many snail species like this sort of bait and are attracted to it. Next morning snails and bait have to be taken out of the tank. This procedure must be repeated regularly; success is better than with mechanical eradications, but this method is not totally, 100% successful.
Biological eradication, using fish: Add snail-eaters, e.g., juvenile Tench (*Tinca tinca*), Clown Loaches (*Botia* spp.), or Puffer Fish to your tank.	Prognosis of success is excellent. Usually these fish remove all snails within a few weeks. Problem: other small co-inhabitants of the aquarium, e.g., neon tetras and guppy males, are not totally safe with 6 inch (15 cm) long tench. Moreover, clown loaches and puffer fish are sometimes a bit rough with other fish, which can cause some restlessness in the tank.
Chemical eradication: Success with various substances available from the aquarium trade	Very successful if applied correctly. Must be repeated in two to three week intervals in order to destroy newly hatched snails also.

Handling Chemicals Correctly

The use of certain chemicals in an aquarium is sometimes unavoidable. For instance, chemicals may have to be used for the eradication of fresh water polyps that have entered the aquarium inadvertently, together with live food. Similarly, to deal effectively with an invasion of snails, as described on page 54, there is sometimes no alternative but to use chemicals.

The Correct Dose
You must always make sure to comply precisely with the instructions of use and dose recommendations from the manufacturer. This applies to the use of chemicals, as well as medications. Giving less than the recommended dose often does not bring the anticipated result. Overdosing can have serious consequences for fish and plants, such as stagnating growth or causing permanent body damage. As soon as the desired result has been obtained from the use of chemicals or medications, do a generous, partial water change (better yet, several such water changes over intervals of several days).

Avoid Chronic Use of Chemicals
In principle, try to avoid giving chemicals and medications routinely every week, hoping that this will achieve a type of permanent prevention solution. In spite of such certainly good intentions, this will achieve exactly the opposite. In fish that have been exposed chronically to some sort of chemical mixture, this will lead inevitably to a permanent weakening of the immune system. Once such chemically affected fish reproduce, their offspring will often show that substantial body damage has occurred;

in many cases this will lead to an early death. Moreover, the body system of a fish tends to get used to medication given on a permanent basis, so that when there is an actual disease outbreak, the medication given will achieve only an unsatisfactory result or none at all. Before you decide to use chemicals in your aquarium, you should at least check whether there may be a biological alternative available with which the same result can be achieved.

As attractive as ramshorn snails may be, they are a nuisance to many aquarium hobbyists, because in an aquarium they tend to reproduce very rapidly.

Fish Diseases: Recognition and Treatment

Unfortunately, even in an optimally cared-for aquarium, it can happen that a fish or two becomes ill. When this happens, it is critically important to be able to quickly diagnose the disease so that the required countermeasures are promptly initiated. Do not make the mistake of trying out all sorts of medications. It is best to consult an experienced aquarist, veterinarian, or the staff of your aquarium shop. It is advantageous if you have a separate tank available for treating sick fish. This same tank can then also be used for quarantine purposes. All newly acquired fish must first be kept in this quarantine tank for two to three weeks before they are put into the main tank. If no disease symptoms develop among the newly acquired fish during this period, they can then be safely transferred to the principal display tank with all the other fish.

The aquarium trade offers effective medication for the treatment of the White Spot Disease that can quickly provide relief for affected specimens.

White Spot Disease

Symptoms: Body and fins covered with tiny white dots. The fish have folded their fins and often swim in laterally swaying motions. They will also rub against the tank decoration or along the bottom. Food is often refused.

Disease organism: The causative organism is the ciliate skin parasite *Ichthyophthirius multifiliis*, which is usually introduced into an aquarium together with newly purchased fish or with live fish food.

Treatment: Even if only a single specimen displays the symptoms, other fish in the same tank are also infected. Therefore all fish must immediately be treated with appropriate medication, available from aquarium and pet shops. Upon completion of treatment, a nutritious diet tends to enhance the healing process.

Velvet Disease

Symptoms: The fish look like they have been "dusted" with icing sugar. The little dots are much smaller than those of the White Spot Disease. The bodies of the fish have a velvety appearance. Respiration is rapid, fins are folded, and the fish swim in a swaying motion. Sometimes, small patches of skin can flake off.

Disease organism: This disease is caused by the flagellate organism *Oodinium pillularis*. It tends to parasitize the skin and gills of fish. This disease is frequently introduced into an aquarium with newly acquired fish.

Treatment: Treatment of this disease is done in a similar fashion as outlined for the White Spot Disease. However, you must make sure that the medication used is specifically for the treatment of the Velvet Disease.

Abdominal Dropsy

Symptoms: The abdominal region of the fish becomes bloated. At the same time, the scales become raised, and in many cases the affected specimens develop "bubble eyes." They often display uncoordinated swimming movements. Internally, dropsy progresses with deterioration of the liver, impaired metabolism, and a bacterial infection.

Treatment: For advanced cases of dropsy there is no effective treatment method. Because of the danger of cross-contamination, remove any diseased specimen from the tank.

Fungus Infections, Mouth Rot, and Fin Rot

Symptoms: Small patches resembling cotton wool and/or "fungus" like coating appear on the body of the affected specimens. At the same time a torulous (bulging) edge develops along the edges of the fins. During the advanced stage of the disease, the fins may become shortened or have completely rotted away.

Disease organisms: Fungi and bacteria, which develop rapidly due to unsatisfactory maintenance (water quality) conditions. Moreover, slowly healing wounds can be secondarily infected by other pathogens.

Treatment: The affected fish must be separated from the main tank population and be treated immediately with appropriate medication (available from aquarium and/or pet shops). In order to improve the physical condition of the fish, they should be given a variable and mainly vitamin-rich diet. A comprehensive water change is also advisable. Upon completion of treatment, the overall aquarium conditions (e.g., water quality) need to be improved.

Handling Chemicals Correctly

TIPS FROM AN
AQUARIUM EXPERT
Axel Gutjahr

SECURITY: All aquarium chemicals and medications must be kept under lock and key in a childproof cabinet.

SUPPLY: Keep only small amounts of chemicals or medication that are relatively quickly used up. Avoid prolonged storage.

STORAGE: If chemicals and medications are labeled "to be stored cool," it is usually still possible to keep them at 64 to 68° F (18 to 20° C). Do not store these substances in a refrigerator together with food items designated for human consumption.

EXPIRATION DATE: Some of these substances have an expiration date. At the time of purchase, make sure that there is still sufficient time for you to use them prior to their expiration date.

APPLICATION: If at all possible, never add medications and aquarium chemicals to the tank simultaneously. Sometimes these substances react with each other and then lose their effectiveness, or produce undesirable side effects.

Problems with Water Plants

When, after a major cleaning, the aquarium is set up again, it can happen that the plants are not really thriving anymore; in fact, they may even start to decline and their growth becomes stunted. There may be various reasons for this.

Possible Causes

When two different plant species are placed too closely to each other, they can be incompatible by nature. The classical examples of this are *Vallisneria* representatives and *Cryptocoryne* species. There is a constant competition between plants, whereby each plant is determined to improve its own survival and reproductive chances, invariably at the expense of other plants. For instance, some plants release substances through their roots that will inhibit the growth of other plants. Again, other plants may exhibit rapid growth and in that process use up the nutrients of their competitors, as well as utilize most of the available light required for photosynthesis. Also, some of the water parameters—such as pH, temperature, and water hardness—may not be ideal for a particular species. Often this manifests itself in reduced growth.

Nutritional Deficiencies

When water plants have been in a particular aquarium for a long period of time where there are relatively few fish, it can come to a general reduction of available plant nutrients. You can resolve the problem quickly through the use of commercially available aquarium fertilizers. When your aquarium plants suddenly develop pale, almost transparent leaves, you are dealing with a *chlorosis*, which is indicative of a lack of iron in the water. The aquarium trade offers various substances with which such an iron deficiency can be eliminated quickly and effectively. Often plants from nurseries where they have been raised immersed become stunted once they are placed fully under water in an aquarium. In fact, often most of the leaves of such plants start to fall off. Unfortunately, there is virtually nothing you can do about it, except for being patient! Plants like that have problems in adapting to the unaccustomed cultivation under water. Usually this phase does not exceed six weeks. Thereafter, these sickly appearing plants, start to regenerate, and soon there will be the first runners or even new plant shoots.

Yellow plant leaves are an indication of an insufficient nutrient supply. Add a moderate amount of fertilizer.

Filter Problems

What do you do when the aquarium filter suddenly loses pumping efficiency or stops working altogether? If this is due to an electrical fault, you have no choice but to get the filter repaired by a qualified repairman; however, it is advisable to get a cost estimate first, because repairs are often more expensive than the price of a new filter.

Do Your Own Minor Repairs

It can happen that the water coming out of a recently cleaned filter-aerator unit only trickles instead of emerging as a powerful stream. The cause of this can be a partial blockage; in addition to aquarium water, pieces of the mat-like filter wool (the filter medium) could have been sucked through the screened opening, located in the upper part of the filter. In this case, you have to open up the filter canister again and pull out the filter wool from the top. Then you smooth it by hand and place it back into the filter, making sure that there are no folds or kinks in the material. If you noticed while the filter was open that the filter wool was indeed properly positioned, there is still the possibility that there is too much air inside the filter. In that case, fill up the entire filter canister (that contains individual filter boxes or chambers, respectively) with water until it overflows. Then replace the upper part of the filter and connect a hose (possibly the one used for siphoning out debris) to the discharge end of the filter pipe. Then, while simultaneously turning on the filter and holding the hose close to your mouth, suck hard on the hose until water comes out. Normally you have to do this only once in order to remove all of the air out of the filter. If, after that, the filter flow is still inadequate, you will have to suck again. If these

This tank shows a very high load of suspended particles that are causing considerable turbidity in the water.

procedures do not produce the desired success, it is advisable to inspect all intake and discharge filter hoses as well as the respective pipe stems. It is possible that some particles have become firmly lodged in the filter system, impeding proper water flow through the filter.

Ruptured Filter Bag

It can happen that the filter bag containing activated charcoal gets torn while it is being cleaned. Until you can get a new bag, you can place charcoal into a nylon stocking and so operate the filter at least on a temporary basis. As an alternative to a filter bag, you can also use a plastic gauze bag, often used for storing soap (available from drugstores and similar shops). In fact, these bags are even suitable for permanent use as filter bags. You can place several such bags inside a filter, each bag containing a different filter medium.

INDEX

Aquarium Associations in the US and Canada

> American Killifish Association
www.aka.org
> American Cichlid Association
P.O. Box 5351
Naperville, IL 60567-5351
> Aquatic Gardeners Association
83 Cathcart St., London
Ontario, Canada N6L 3L9
> International Betta Congress
923 Wadsworth St.
Syracuse, NY 13208-2419
> North American Discus Society
6939 Justin Drive, Mississauga,
Ontario, Canada, L4T 1M4
> American Livebearer Association
Timothy J. Brady,
Membership Chairman
5 Zerbe Street
Cressona, PA 17929-1513
tjbrady@fast.net
> Federation of American Aquarium
Societies (FAAS)
Hedy Padgett (Membership Chair)
4816 E. 64th Street
Indianapolis, IN 46220-4728

Important Notice

> The electrical equipment items described in this book for use in conjunction with aquariums must carry official safety certification

> Be aware of the inherent dangers when working with electrical equipment, cables, and conduit, especially when in the proximity of water.

> Installation of an earth leakage (fault current) circuit breaker is recommended.

Local Aquarium Clubs

> Virtually every town and city in the United States has at least one (and often more) aquarium club. For details, check the local telephone directory or search the Internet.

Questions about all aquarium-related topics (fishkeeping, water plants, fish diseases, aquarium equipment, basic water chemistry, etc.) can be directed at your local aquarium or specialist pet shop staff. There are also numerous aquarium forum sites available on the Internet, which deal with all aquarium topics.

Aquarium Insurance

> For third-party, liability, and personal injury insurance, contact the major insurance companies in your area.

Aquarium Magazines & Journals

> Tropical Fish Hobbyist
TFH Publications, Inc.
Neptune, NJ
> Freshwater & Marine Aquarium
(FAMA)
view online at
www.fishchannel.com
> Practical Fishkeeping (UK)
subscribe at *www.*
practicalfishkeeping.co.uk

Aquarium Books

> Goldstein, Robert J. *Marine Reef Aquarium Handbook*. Barron's Educational Series, Inc., 2008.
> Gutjahr, Axel. *Setting Up Themed Aquariums*. Barron's Educational Series, Inc., 2008.

> Hiscock, Peter. *Aquarium Designs Inspired by Nature*. Barron's Educational Series, Inc., 2003.
> ———. *Aquarium Plants*. Barron's Educational Series, Inc., 2005.
> Tullock, John. *Your First Marine Aquarium*. Barron's Educational Series, Inc., 2008.
> Tunze, Axel. *Saltwater Aquarium*. Barron's Educational Series, Inc., 2001.

Photo credits

Aquapress: 13, 23 (top left), 23 (center right), 23 (bottom); Blickwinkel: 31 (center); Werner Eigelshofen: 39 (bottom); Oliver Giel: 7, 12, 14, 15 (right), 17, 20, 30/31, 48, 49; Giese-mann-Aquaristik: 8; Axel Gutjahr: 10 (top), 39 (center); Andreas Hartl: 38 (top); Imago: 43; Burkard Kahl: 1, 2 (left), 3, 4, 9, 11, 19, 22 (top), 22 (bottom left), 23 (bottom right), 24, 27-1, 27-2, 27-3, 34 (center), 36 (top), 36 (center), 36 (bottom), 37 (top), 37 (center), 39 (top), 44, 46, 50, 58, 59; Ingo Koslowski: 15 (left), 56; Horst Linke: 41; Peter Lukas: 30 (top left), 40, 51, 52; A. van den Niewenhuizen: 38 (center), 55; Okapia: 31 (bottom), 53 (right); Armin Peither: 29, 31 (top right), 34 (top), 35 (top), 37 (bottom); Reinhard-Tierfoto: 23 (center), 30 (top right), 30 (bottom); Gunther Schmida: 38 (bottom); Heinz Schmidbauer: 2 (right), 10 (bottom), 32, 34 (bottom), 42-1, 42-2, 45, 53 (left); Wolfgang Staeck: 35 (bottom); Uwe Werner: 16, 35 (center)

The title of the German book is *Das
Aquarium*
English translation by U. Erich Friese

All inquiries should be addressed to:
Barron's Educational Series, Inc.
250 Wireless Boulevard
Hauppauge, New York 11788
www.barronseduc.com

ISBN-13: 978-0-7641-3944-4
ISBN-10: 0-7641-3944-4

Library of Congress Control No.: 2007937208

Printed in China
9 8 7 6 5 4 3 2 1

The Author

Axel Gutjahr has been enthusias-
tic about keeping and breeding
fish since childhood. This passion
carried over into his university
studies in animal reproduction
and agricultural economics. Apart
from his involvement with tropical
fish, he is also interested in a
variety of coldwater fish species
and their care in garden ponds. In
the field of aquarium keeping,
Axel Gutjahr is also the author of
several successful books and
numerous articles, published in
various aquarium journals and
periodicals.

SOS—What to Do?

Water is coming out of a side corner of the tank.

Immediately: Lower the water level to a point below where the water seems to be coming out. If possible, repair with silicon sealant. **Long-term:** If the damage cannot be repaired, a new tank will have to be purchased.

Heater fails during the winter months.

Immediately: Increase the room temperature, ideally by means of central heating. **Long-term:** Repair the old heater or buy a new one. Please note: Heaters must only be repaired by licensed electricians or other qualified servicemen.

There are dead fish floating in the tank every day.

Immediately: Remove any dead fish from the tank. You are probably dealing with an epidemic disease that must be treated appropriately. **Long-term:** Start feeding only quality, vitamin-enriched food. This will enhance the healing process.

The fish are "gasping" for air at the surface.

Immediately: Increase aeration to maximum level. Initiate water change, whereby 80 to 90 percent of the tank water is replaced with conditioned freshwater. Monitor the water temperature. With an aquarium heater failure, the tank water may have become extremely warm. In such a case, turn off the heater and float some ice cubes in the tank. **Long-term:** Thoroughly investigate the cause of the problem, e.g., by reducing the fish inventory or replacing the substrate (and so remove any areas of decay in the sand). Initiate a comprehensive and thorough cleaning of the tank. If a defective heater caused the problem, it will need to be repaired or be replaced with a new one.

One of the bamboo sticks shows an area of decay.

Immediately: Remove the stick from the aquarium. Either cut off the affected area with a knife or saw, or dispose of the bamboo stick altogether. **Long-term:** Check and, if need be, re-seal all cut surfaces on the bamboo sticks with silicon sealant to keep out any decay-causing bacteria or fungi.